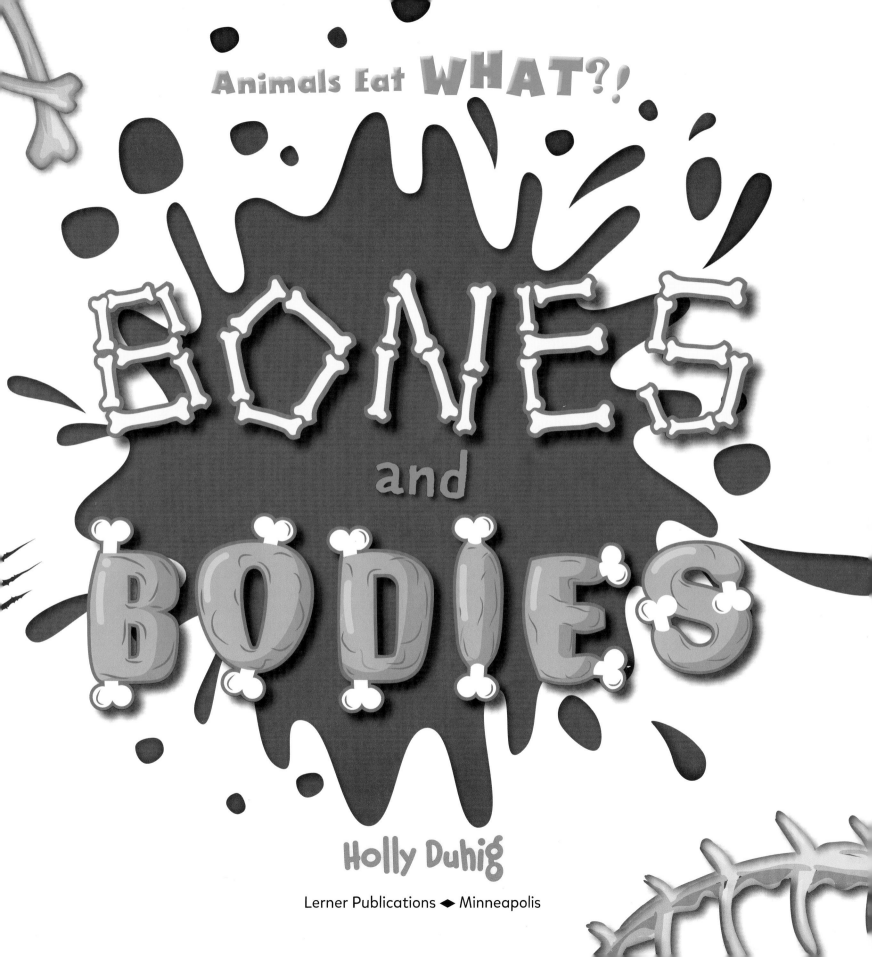

# Animals Eat WHAT?!

# BONES and BODIES

## Holly Duhig

Lerner Publications ◆ Minneapolis

First American edition published in 2020 by Lerner Publishing Group, Inc.

Editor: Emilie Dufresne
Design: Jasmine Porter

Lerner Publications Company
An imprint of Lerner Publishing Group, Inc.
241 First Avenue North
Minneapolis, MN 55401 USA

For reading levels and more information, look up this title at www.lernerbooks.com.

Main body text set in VAG Rounded Std. Typeface provided by Adobe Systems.

Photo credits:
Images are courtesy of Shutterstock.com, with thanks to Getty Images, Thinkstock Photo, and iStockphoto. Freddy the Fly: Natthapon Boochagorn & Roi and Roi. Front cover: BeRad, MaryValery, KittyVector, VectorShow, YoPixArt. 2: Alfmaler. 5: Kletr, Eric Isselee, StockSmartStart, PiXXart, r.classen. 6: Alfmaler. 7: MicheleB. 8: David Havel. 10: Alta Oosthuizen. 11: NataliaVo. 12: Vickey Chauhan. 13: lady-luck. 14: Inked Pixels. By Linda Snook, National Oceanic and Atmospheric Administration (NOAA) / Cordell Bank National Marine Sanctuary (CBNMS) - http://www.photolib.noaa.gov/htmls/sanc1692.htm http://www.photolib.noaa.gov/bigs/sanc1692.jpg, Public Domain, https://commons.wikimedia.org/w/index.php?curid=8984320. 15: Sunflowerr. 16: Tanya Puntti. 17: angkrit. 18: Holger Kirk. 19: Krisana Antharith. 20: Jurgens Potgieter. 21: SCOTTCHAN, xpixel. 22: spline_x, Ron Vargas. 23: judyjump.

Library of Congress Cataloging-in-Publication Data

Names: Duhig, Holly, author.
Title: Bones and bodies / Holly Duhig.
Description: Minneapolis : Lerner Publications, 2020. | Series: Animals eat what? | Includes index. | Audience: Ages 6–10 | Audience: Grades 2–3 | Summary: "Do animals really eat bones and bodies? They sure do! Full-color photography and funny facts will engage young readers in learning about the biological processes of living things"— Provided by publisher.
Identifiers: LCCN 2019028044 (print) | LCCN 2019028045 (ebook) | ISBN 9781541579323 (library binding) | ISBN 9781541587045 (paperback) | ISBN 9781541582583 (ebook pdf)
Subjects: LCSH: Scavengers (Zoology)—Juvenile literature. | Animals—Food—Juvenile literature.
Classification: LCC QL756.5 .D84 2020  (print) | LCC QL756.5  (ebook) | DDC 591.5/3—dc23

LC record available at https://lccn.loc.gov/2019028044
LC ebook record available at https://lccn.loc.gov/2019028045

Manufactured in the United States of America
1-47214-47919-7/16/2019

# Contents

WORDS THAT LOOK LIKE THIS CAN BE FOUND IN THE GLOSSARY ON PAGE 24.

# Animals Eat what?!

All animals need to eat food to stay alive. However, some animals have different ideas about what counts as "food."

IT IS I, FREDDY THE FLY, WORLD-FAMOUS CRITIC OF UNUSUAL FOOD!

I CAN'T WAIT TO TASTE SOME OF THE DELICIOUS DISHES THE ANIMAL KINGDOM HAS TO OFFER. FLIES AREN'T PICKY EATERS!

MOSQUITOS DRINK BLOOD.

RACCOONS EAT FROM TRASH CANS.

DUNG BEETLES EAT POOP.

# Banquet of Bones

As a human, you've probably never gnawed on a juicy bone or feasted on roadkill, but for many animals, dead bodies are an important part of their everyday <u>diet</u>.

Animals that kill other animals for their meat are called predators. Animals that eat things that are already dead, or have been killed by predators, are called scavengers.

SCAVENGERS

LOTS OF ANIMALS ARE SCAVENGERS, INCLUDING FLIES LIKE ME! SOME SAY WE ARE LAZY, BUT IT GIVES US MORE TIME TO DO OTHER THINGS, LIKE SLEEPING.

ZZZ

# Vile Vultures

Vultures are famous scavengers. They are experts at finding the remains of animals that predators have left behind.

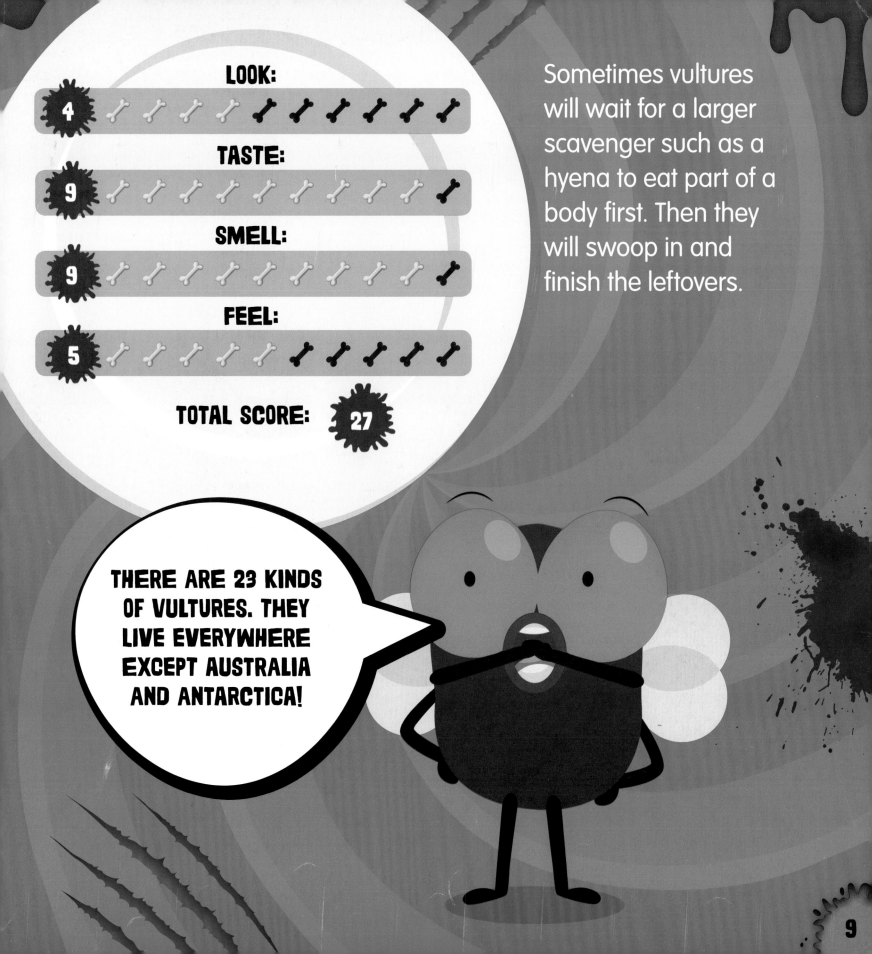

# Bone Bashers

Bearded vultures are scavengers too. However, instead of eating the bodies of animals, they eat the bones! Bearded vultures love bone marrow, which is found inside bones.

To break apart bigger bones, they will fly high and drop them onto rocks. The bones break open, and the vultures can get to the bone marrow.

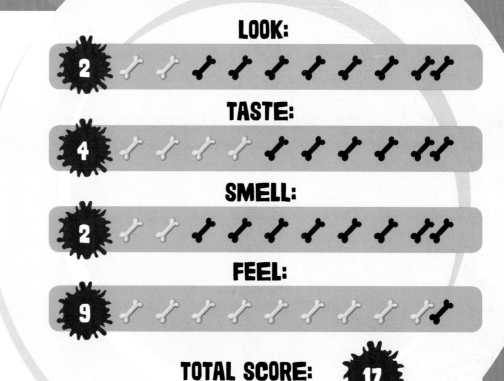

LOOK: 2

TASTE: 4

SMELL: 2

FEEL: 9

TOTAL SCORE: 17

MMM, CRUNCHY ON THE OUTSIDE, SOFT IN THE MIDDLE.

THAT'S MINE!

# Hungry Hyenas

Out on the African savanna, there are lots of hungry scavengers to help clean up after the predators. Striped hyenas are one of the larger scavengers.

Striped hyenas will eat the <u>flesh</u> of zebras, wildebeests, and gazelles. If there is not much meat left, they will munch on the bones instead. Some hyena mothers bring bones back for their cubs.

HYENAS HAVE BEEN KNOWN TO EAT HUMAN BODIES AFTER BATTLES!

LOOK:
1

TASTE:
8

SMELL:
7

FEEL:
7

TOTAL SCORE: 23

# Flesh-Eating Fish

Hagfish are worm-like fish that live deep underwater on the seafloor. They live here so they can feed on dead fish that sink to the bottom of the ocean.

There is not always a steady supply of sinking sea creatures, so hagfish make the most of every snack. They can take in <u>nutrients</u> through their skin and <u>gills</u> as well as their mouths.

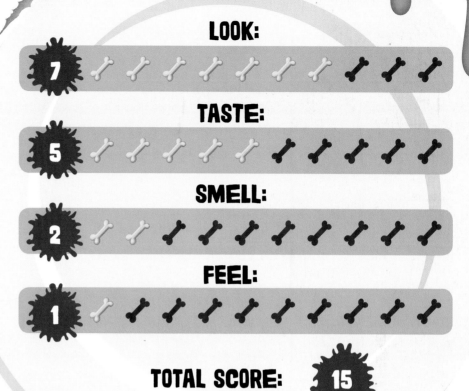

LOOK: 7

TASTE: 5

SMELL: 2

FEEL: 1

TOTAL SCORE: 15

HAGFISH CAN CREATE GROSS SLIME TO KEEP PREDATORS AWAY.

# Devilish Diners

Tasmanian devils live on the island of Tasmania. They'll eat almost anything, but their favorite meal is flesh.

There isn't a body part that the Tasmanian devil can't handle. It has a bite so powerful it can break through metal, so fur and bones are no problem!

HEY! LEAVE SOME FOR ME!

TASMANIAN DEVILS WOULD RATHER EAT WASHED-UP DEAD FISH THAN HUNT FOR FISH THEMSELVES.

LOOK:

5

TASTE:

10

SMELL:

10

FEEL:

10

TOTAL SCORE:
35

# Munching Maggots

Maggots are the <u>larvae</u> of flies. Flies lay their eggs inside the body of something that has recently died. When the maggots hatch, they have plenty to eat.

SCIENTISTS CAN WORK OUT HOW LONG SOMETHING HAS BEEN DEAD BY THE AGE OF THE MAGGOTS FEEDING ON THE BODY.

As maggots wriggle through their meal, their bodies produce a liquid that breaks down the flesh around them.

LOOK AT MY BABIES GO! THIS MEAL REALLY TAKES ME BACK TO MY YOUNGER YEARS.

LOOK:
10

TASTE:
10

SMELL:
10

FEEL:
10

TOTAL SCORE: 40

# Skull Snackers

If you thought these gentle giants just ate plants all day, then think again. Giraffes have been known to eat bones for breakfast! They've even been spotted munching on buffalo skulls.

LOOK:

0

TASTE:

0

SMELL:

0

FEEL:

1

TOTAL SCORE: 1

Giraffes don't hunt animals. They just gnaw on bones they come across. Giraffes chew on bones for important nutrients that they don't get from their usual diet.

HMM, THERE DOESN'T SEEM TO BE MUCH TO THIS.

# Do You Eat Bones?

Gelatin is an ingredient in many foods including marshmallows and gummy candy.

**GELATIN**

Gelatin is made from animal parts such as skin, cartilage, and even… You guessed it!

# BONES!

VEGETARIANS ARE PEOPLE WHO DON'T EAT MEAT. MANY VEGETARIANS DON'T EAT GUMMY CANDY BECAUSE THE GELATIN IN THEM IS MADE FROM ANIMALS.

THERE'S NO BONES ABOUT IT, MARSHMALLOWS ARE DELICIOUS!

LOOK:

10

TASTE:

10

SMELL:

10

FEEL:

1

TOTAL SCORE:  31

# Glossary

| | |
|---|---|
| **CARTILAGE** | a flexible tissue found in joints and other places around the body |
| **CRITIC** | someone whose job it is to judge something, such as food |
| **DIET** | the kinds of food that a person or animal usually eats |
| **FLESH** | the soft tissue of a body |
| **GILLS** | body parts that some animals use to breathe underwater |
| **LARVAE** | a type of young insect that grows and changes before it becomes an adult |
| **NUTRIENTS** | things that plants and animals need to grow and stay healthy |

# Index